sweet scoops

sweet
scoops

recipes   **Shelly Kaldunski**

photographs   **Thayer Allyson Gowdy**

weldon**owen**

contents

i scream, you scream...

For most of us, our fondest memories of enjoying ice cream are from childhood. They include balmy summer nights, the jingle of an ice cream truck, the sand and the sun, neighborhood walks, and family and friends. If the ice cream was made at home, it was an all-day event involving a big wooden bucket, bags of rock salt, and lots of elbow grease to churn out a delicious frozen treat.

Today, with the new electric machines, making ice cream doesn't have to take all day, and it's not just a dessert for kids. Along with other frozen confections like gelato, sorbet, and granita, ice cream has gained sophistication over the past few years. It has found its way onto fancy restaurant menus, where a variety of scoops are offered à la carte, or sorbets and granitas are served as palate cleansers between courses and as lighter dessert options during the warm months.

In this book, we begin with recipes for the best of the classic ice cream and gelato flavors, such as Vanilla Bean, Strawberry, and Espresso Ice Creams and Pistachio Gelato. Then, we draw on the recent trend toward creative flavors by offering recipes for what we call modern ice creams and gelatos. These include twists on classic flavors, like Salted Caramel Ice Cream and Mascarpone-Hazelnut Gelato, or ice creams featuring unexpected ingredients, as in Lavender Ice Cream with Honeyed Pine Nuts, Meyer Lemon–Olive Oil Ice Cream, or Jasmine Tea Ice Cream with Chocolate Slivers.

Recipes for creamy sherbets, soft frozen yogurts, and refreshing sorbets and granitas—along with a chapter covering cones, cookies, sauces, and toppings—complete this frozen dessert–lovers' recipe collection. These are treats that everyone will love.

modern flavors

Boutique-like ice cream shops and gelaterias, now opening across the United States, are playing with creative flavor combinations. Using the highest-quality dairy products, these shops make the classic flavors as well as some with surprising ingredients, such as avocado, passion fruit, basil, sea salt, curry powder, and tea.

ice cream styles

French-style, or custard-style, ice cream is often called classic ice cream. Egg yolks, cream, and flavorings are cooked to make a custard, which is then churned and frozen in an ice cream maker. Philadelphia-style ice cream is made without egg yolks, so it's less rich than French-style ice cream. The lighter base works especially well for fruit ice creams because the fresh flavors of the fruit can shine through. Other ice creams that have emulsifiers as ingredients, like peanut butter, are also often made without egg yolks.

the scoop on the scoops

The presence or absence of a dairy product, or even the type of dairy used, can mean the difference between sorbet and sherbet or ice cream and gelato. Here's a guide to help you decipher the terms.

ICE CREAM Traditional ice cream is made from a mixture of a dairy product (cream or a mixture of milk and cream), a sweetener (usually granulated or brown sugar), and flavorings (like chocolate, fruit, or nuts). Many ice creams contain egg yolks (see sidebar at left).

GELATO Soft and creamy, this Italian-style treat is traditionally made with milk, not cream, and egg yolks, though some versions include cream and exclude eggs. The signature silky texture of gelato is due less to the ingredients used and more to the way it is churned, in a machine that incorporates less air and freezes at a higher temperature than an ice cream maker.

FROZEN YOGURT & SHERBET Frozen yogurt is a softer, tangier alternative to ice cream. It can be made using non-fat, low-fat, or full-fat yogurt. For creamier results, you can also use Greek-style yogurt, which is higher in fat than plain yogurt. Sherbet is made with a base of fruit purée and sugar to which a dairy product, such as buttermilk or cream, is added for creaminess.

SORBET Sorbet is usually made with a mixture of a fruit purée, water, and sugar, which can then be frozen in a standard ice cream maker. Because sorbet has few other ingredients, the flavor is often quite intense.

GRANITA & ICE Granita is an Italian-style dessert made with a sugar syrup and flavorings that is frozen in a shallow pan. During the freezing process, it is scraped periodically with a fork to create a granular texture. Flavored ices are similar to granitas, but are often finer in texture. Both granitas and ices can be frozen into ice pops (see page 80) or ice cubes.

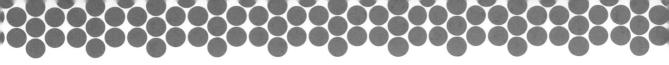

more than the sum of its parts

Since they use so few ingredients, the best frozen treats are made with the finest ingredients you can find. When possible, try to use organic dairy products, seasonal fruits, and quality spices and liqueurs.

MILK, CREAM & EGGS In these recipes, the ratio of whole milk to heavy cream is important so that the resulting texture is creamy, but not too heavy. In some cases, ingredients such as crème fraîche or mascarpone cheese contribute creaminess, too, so the quantity of cream in the recipe is reduced. Egg yolks give French-style ice cream and gelato a luxurious mouthfeel. All of the recipes in this book use large grade A eggs. Avoid using extra-large or jumbo eggs, since they have significantly larger yolks and can throw off the results of the recipes.

FRUIT Fresh, seasonal fruits are delicious in ice creams, gelatos, frozen yogurts, and sherbets. Some fruits have high water contents and can sometimes, if not cooked first or if added in excess, make frozen desserts overly icy. Cooking the fruit first reduces the amount of water added and concentrates the flavors—it's also a good way to make the most of not-quite-ripe fruits. If fruits are out of season, use high-quality, unsweetened frozen fruits.

CHOCOLATE, NUTS & OTHER FLAVORINGS Choose the best chocolate you can find; it will be creamier when melted than some lower-quality brands and will not contribute a waxy mouthfeel. Buy nuts whole and in bulk at a store where the product turnover is high. Toast or grind the nuts up to a few hours before you make the ice cream. Also, look for vanilla beans that are soft and pliable, not stiff and dry. For smooth ice creams with subtle flavor, ingredients like nuts or coffee beans are heated with the cream (and/or milk), and then removed when the cooked custard is strained. Chunkier mix-ins are often added at the end of churning.

sweeteners

Sugar plays a role in all of the frozen treats in this book. Using the right amount of sugar is crucial: too much can inhibit freezing, making ice creams too soft and granitas slushy. For French-style ice cream, sugar is whisked with egg yolks and then dissolves during the cooking of the custard. Brown sugar is sometimes used in place of granulated sugar for a deeper flavor. Flavored sugar syrups are the bases for all the granitas and ices. Corn syrup, used in sherbets, adds creaminess and compensates for the lack of butterfat in the recipe.

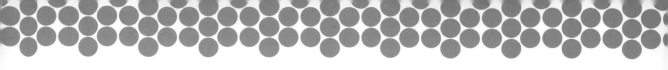

scoops & paddles

There is a wide variety of ice cream scoops available on the market, from the traditional no-frills metal scoops to those with release levers and some that allow you to fill the handle with water to make scooping easier. You can find most tools in a variety of sizes. Specialty paddles, used in Italy to serve gelato, are available at kitchenware stores. These can be used to present a variety of frozen desserts in a more casual way—just pressed onto a plate or into a bowl. All types of ice cream tools benefit from a dip in cool water before scooping.

tools of the trade

Depending on your budget, how often you make churned frozen desserts, and the desired quality and quantity of the finished product, there are many types of ice cream machines available. Most machines will also make gelato, frozen yogurt, and sorbet.

MANUAL ICE CREAM MAKER This type of ice cream maker uses a hand crank to rotate a steel can that rests inside a large wooden bucket. A mixture of ice and rock salt is added to the space between the bucket and the steel can; the crank is then turned by hand for 20–40 minutes. It's a great way to get kids involved in the process of making ice cream and since there's no cover, you can even let them taste the mixture after they've tried turning the crank. An electric model in the same style is also available.

ELECTRIC ICE CREAM MAKER The simplest of these machines is lightweight and comes with a canister that needs to be prefrozen for at least 24 hours before you use it. If you make ice cream often, it's a good idea to purchase two canisters so you can always have one ready to go in the freezer. Also, for some models of stand mixers, you can purchase a special ice cream paddle and freezable mixer bowl to make frozen desserts. More complex electric machines are equipped with built-in compression freezers, so they are ready to churn at any time and can make batches of frozen desserts continuously. A temperature-control gauge ensures creamy, smooth results.

GELATO MAKER The primary difference between ice cream and gelato is in the way each is churned. Gelato makers freeze mixtures at a temperature that is 10–20 degrees warmer than ice cream makers. They also incorporate less air while churning, giving gelato its signature smooth, creamy texture. Unlike ice cream, gelato is best served in its soft state, directly after churning, but it can also be stored, covered, in a freezer for up to 3 days.

whipping up a batch

PREPARING THE BASE The hands-on preparation time for frozen desserts is short, but there are some steps that are essential to achieving the best texture and flavor in the final product. Many recipes start by cooking a base of some kind, such as a custard or a fruit-sugar mixture. As soon as the base is finished cooking, it is important to cool it in an ice bath either to stop the cooking of the eggs (if making a French-style ice cream base) or to keep the fruit mixture vibrant and fresh-tasting (if making a sorbet or granita base). Before churning, the cooled base must be chilled in the refrigerator until it is very cold, at least 4 hours. If the base is too warm when you add it to the ice cream maker, it will take longer to freeze and too much air will be incorporated, affecting the dessert's texture and flavor.

CHURNING To churn a frozen dessert, add the cold dessert base to the ice cream maker. Depending on the manufacturer and model, the churning will take 20–40 minutes (consult the manufacturer's instructions for specifics). When it's done, you can either serve the dessert freshly spun for a softer texture, or freeze it for at least 2 hours for firmer, scoopable results.

STORING To store, spoon the freshly churned frozen dessert or finished granita into a 1- to 1½-quart freezer-safe container. Cover freshly churned desserts with parchment or waxed paper, pressing it directly onto the surface to prevent ice crystals from forming. Store in the freezer for up to 3 days.

SERVING When ready to serve, if the frozen dessert is extremely firm, place it in the refrigerator for about 20 minutes to soften; this helps with scooping and heightens the flavors. Granitas and ices are typically served slightly thawed and slushy, so take them out of the freezer about 5 minutes before you plan to serve them. One quart of most frozen desserts will make 6–8 servings. One quart of granita or ice serves about 4.

troubleshooting

● Wine, liqueur, and other types of alcohol add bold flavor to frozen desserts. Avoid using more than is called for in the recipe, as alcohol can inhibit freezing.

● Swirling fresh fruit, nuts, candy, or other ingredients into frozen desserts gives them bursts of flavor and a nice texture, but cut the pieces small so they don't interfere with the freezing process.

● To keep desserts colder for longer, especially in hot weather, first place the serving dishes in the freezer for about an hour until they are very cold.

classic ice creams & gelatos

vanilla bean ice cream

Steeping the vanilla bean pod and its seeds in the cream gives this recipe an intense vanilla flavor and a classic speckled appearance. For a more old fashioned–style ice cream, make a Smooth Vanilla variation by replacing the vanilla bean with 1 tablespoon high-quality vanilla extract.

2 cups half-and-half

1 1/2 cups heavy cream

1 vanilla bean, split in half lengthwise, seeds scraped (page 105)

8 large egg yolks

3/4 cup sugar

1/4 teaspoon salt

MAKES ABOUT 1 1/2 QUARTS

strawberry-vanilla cups

Make a sophisticated sundae by filling Waffle Cups (page 87) with quartered strawberries, then topping them with a scoop of ice cream. If desired, top with Hot Fudge Sauce (page 92).

In a heavy saucepan, combine the half-and-half, cream, and vanilla bean pod and seeds. Warm over medium-high heat, stirring occasionally, until the mixture barely comes to a simmer, about 5 minutes. Meanwhile, in a heatproof bowl, combine the egg yolks, sugar, and salt. Whisk vigorously until the mixture lightens in color and doubles in volume, about 2 minutes.

Remove the cream mixture from the heat. Whisking constantly, slowly pour about 1 cup of the warm cream mixture into the egg mixture and whisk until smooth. Pour the resulting egg-cream mixture back into the saucepan, whisking constantly, and place over medium heat. Using a wooden spoon, stir until the mixture forms a custard thick enough to coat the back of the spoon (page 103), 1–2 minutes. Do not let it boil.

Meanwhile, set up an ice bath (page 103) in a large bowl and nest a smaller heatproof bowl inside. Pour the custard through a fine-mesh sieve into the smaller bowl. Discard the vanilla bean. Stir the custard occasionally until cool. Remove the bowl from the ice bath and cover with plastic wrap. Refrigerate until very cold, at least 4 hours or up to 3 days.

Pour the cold custard into an ice cream maker and churn according to the manufacturer's instructions. Spoon the ice cream into a freezer-safe container and place parchment or waxed paper directly on the surface. Cover tightly and freeze until firm, at least 2 hours or up to 3 days.

chocolate ice cream

Using high-quality chocolate makes this ice cream rich in flavor and creamy in texture. Look for a bar with 70 percent cocoa solids; the higher the cocoa content, the more intense the flavor. Low-quality chocolate has a waxy coating and won't achieve the desired smooth mouthfeel.

2 cups heavy cream

1½ cups whole milk

7 large egg yolks

¾ cup sugar

¼ cup unsweetened cocoa powder

¼ teaspoon salt

7 ounces bittersweet chocolate such as Scharffen Berger, Valrhona, or Callebaut, finely chopped

2 teaspoons vanilla extract

MAKES ABOUT 1½ QUARTS

In a heavy saucepan, combine the cream and milk. Warm over medium-high heat, stirring occasionally, until the mixture barely comes to a simmer, about 5 minutes. Meanwhile, in a heatproof bowl, combine the egg yolks, sugar, cocoa powder, and salt. Whisk vigorously until the mixture doubles in volume, about 2 minutes.

Remove the cream mixture from the heat. Whisking constantly, slowly pour about 1 cup of the warm cream mixture into the egg mixture and whisk until smooth. Pour the resulting egg-cream mixture back into the saucepan, whisking constantly, and place over medium heat. Add the chopped chocolate and vanilla to the saucepan. Using a wooden spoon, stir until the chocolate melts and the mixture forms a custard thick enough to coat the back of the spoon (page 103), 1–2 minutes. Do not let it boil.

Meanwhile, set up an ice bath (page 103) in a large bowl and nest a smaller heatproof bowl inside. Pour the custard through a fine-mesh sieve into the smaller bowl; stir occasionally until cool. Remove the bowl from the ice bath and cover with plastic wrap. Refrigerate until very cold, at least 4 hours or up to 3 days.

Pour the cold custard into an ice cream maker and churn according to the manufacturer's instructions. Spoon the ice cream into a freezer-safe container and place parchment or waxed paper directly on the surface. Cover tightly and freeze until firm, at least 2 hours or up to 3 days.

espresso ice cream

Even though the custard in this recipe is strained, bits of ground espresso make their way through the sieve, giving the ice cream a welcome crunch. For a smooth variation, replace the ground coffee with 1/4 cup whole espresso beans; strain them out when you strain the cooked custard.

1¾ cups heavy cream

1½ cups whole milk

2 tablespoons ground espresso

4 large egg yolks

½ cup plus 2 tablespoons sugar

¼ teaspoon salt

MAKES ABOUT 1 QUART

In a heavy saucepan, combine the cream, milk, and espresso. Warm over medium-high heat, stirring occasionally, until the mixture barely comes to a simmer, about 5 minutes. Meanwhile, in a heatproof bowl, combine the egg yolks, sugar, and salt. Whisk vigorously until the mixture lightens in color and doubles in volume, about 2 minutes.

Remove the cream mixture from the heat. Whisking constantly, slowly pour about 1 cup of the warm cream mixture into the egg mixture and whisk until smooth. Pour the resulting egg-cream mixture back into the saucepan, whisking constantly, and place over medium heat. Using a wooden spoon, stir until the mixture forms a custard thick enough to coat the back of the spoon (page 103), 1–2 minutes. Do not let it boil.

Meanwhile, set up an ice bath (page 103) in a large bowl and nest a smaller heatproof bowl inside. Pour the custard through a fine-mesh sieve into the smaller bowl; stir occasionally until cool. Remove the bowl from the ice bath and cover with plastic wrap. Refrigerate until very cold, at least 4 hours or up to 3 days.

Pour the cold custard into an ice cream maker and churn according to the manufacturer's instructions. Spoon the ice cream into a freezer-safe container and place parchment or waxed paper directly on the surface. Cover tightly and freeze until firm, at least 2 hours or up to 3 days.

strawberry ice cream

This recipe combines the richness of a custard-based ice cream with the vibrancy of fresh strawberries, which are brightened with a touch of lemon juice. Crushing the berries instead of puréeing them creates juicy bits of strawberry flavor in each bite of ice cream.

3 cups strawberries (1½ pints), hulled and cut in half

⅔ cup plus 2 tablespoons sugar

2 teaspoons fresh lemon juice

1 cup heavy cream

1 cup half-and-half

3 large egg yolks

Pinch salt

MAKES ABOUT 1½ QUARTS

double-strawberry sundaes

For a real springtime treat, top this ice cream with Fresh Strawberry Topping (page 95) and a dollop of crème fraîche or Vanilla Whipped Cream (page 79).

In a bowl, combine the berries, the 2 tablespoons sugar, and the lemon juice and lightly crush with a fork. Cover and let stand for about 1 hour.

In a heavy saucepan, combine the heavy cream and half-and-half. Warm over medium-high heat, stirring occasionally, until the mixture barely comes to a simmer, about 5 minutes. Meanwhile, in a heatproof bowl, combine the egg yolks, the remaining ⅔ cup sugar, and the salt. Whisk vigorously until the mixture lightens in color and doubles in volume, about 2 minutes.

Remove the cream mixture from the heat. Whisking constantly, slowly pour about 1 cup of the warm cream mixture into the egg mixture and whisk until smooth. Pour the resulting egg-cream mixture back into the saucepan, whisking constantly, and place over medium heat. Using a wooden spoon, stir until the mixture forms a custard thick enough to coat the back of the spoon (page 103), 1–2 minutes. Do not let it boil.

Meanwhile, set up an ice bath (page 103) in a large bowl and nest a smaller heatproof bowl inside. Pour the custard through a fine-mesh sieve into the smaller bowl; stir occasionally until cool. Remove the bowl from the ice bath, stir in the strawberry mixture, and cover with plastic wrap. Refrigerate until very cold, at least 4 hours or up to 1 day.

Pour the cold custard into an ice cream maker and churn according to the manufacturer's instructions. Spoon the ice cream into a freezer-safe container and place parchment or waxed paper directly on the surface. Cover tightly and freeze until firm, at least 2 hours or up to 3 days.

pistachio gelato

Toasting the pistachios before they are steeped in the milk accentuates the flavor of the delicate nuts in the finished gelato. To toast them, place the shelled pistachios in a single layer on a rimmed baking sheet and bake in a preheated 350°F oven until fragrant, about 10 minutes.

5 cups whole milk

2 cups unsalted shelled pistachios, toasted (see above) and coarsely chopped

10 large egg yolks

1½ cups sugar

¼ teaspoon salt

1 teaspoon almond extract

2–3 drops green food coloring (optional)

MAKES ABOUT 1½ QUARTS

pistachio gelato pops

To make fun single servings, use a 1½-inch scoop to form small rounds of firm gelato and place them on a parchment-lined baking sheet. Insert a craft stick about 1 inch into each scoop, then carefully dip the lower halves of the pops in toasted chopped pistachios. Freeze until ready to serve.

In a heavy saucepan, combine the milk and toasted pistachios. Warm over medium-high heat, stirring occasionally, until the mixture barely comes to a simmer, about 5 minutes. Meanwhile, in a heatproof bowl, combine the egg yolks, sugar, and salt. Whisk vigorously until the mixture lightens in color and doubles in volume, about 2 minutes.

Remove the milk mixture from the heat. Whisking constantly, slowly pour about 1 cup of the warm milk mixture into the egg mixture and whisk until smooth. Pour the resulting egg-milk mixture back into the saucepan, whisking constantly, and place over medium heat. Using a wooden spoon, stir until the mixture forms a custard thick enough to coat the back of the spoon (page 103), 1–2 minutes. Do not let it boil.

Meanwhile, set up an ice bath (page 103) in a large bowl and nest a smaller heatproof bowl inside. Pour the custard through a fine-mesh sieve into the smaller bowl; stir occasionally until cool. Remove the bowl from the ice bath; stir in the almond extract and food coloring, if using; and cover with plastic wrap. Refrigerate until very cold, at least 4 hours or up to 3 days.

Pour the cold custard into an ice cream maker and churn according to the manufacturer's instructions. Serve right away or spoon the gelato into a freezer-safe container and place parchment or waxed paper directly on the surface. Cover tightly and freeze until firm, at least 2 hours or up to 3 days.

peach–raspberry swirl ice cream

An ode to Peach Melba, this ice cream says "summer is here." To intensify the color of the ice cream, add a few whole fresh raspberries to the peach-cream mixture while you are puréeing it in the blender; the ice cream base will turn a deeper shade of peach.

1 cup raspberries

¼ cup raspberry jam or preserves

¾ cup sugar

1¼ pounds peaches (about 4), halved and pitted

1 cup heavy cream

⅓ cup crème fraîche

¼ teaspoon salt

MAKES ABOUT 1½ QUARTS

Combine the raspberries and jam in a bowl. Using a fork, mash the berries to create a chunky mixture. Cover and refrigerate until ready to use.

In a large frying pan deep enough to fit the peach halves comfortably, combine the sugar and ¾ cup water. Bring to a boil over medium-high heat, stirring occasionally, until the sugar is completely dissolved, about 5 minutes. Add the peaches, cut sides down, reduce the heat to low, and simmer for 5 minutes. Turn the peaches over and continue to cook for about 2 minutes longer, or until the fruit softens and the skins begin to loosen. Remove from the heat and let cool to room temperature. Remove the skins from the peaches and discard.

Spoon the peaches and their cooking liquid into a blender or food processor and add the cream, crème fraîche, and salt. Purée until the mixture is completely smooth. Pour the mixture into a bowl and cover with plastic wrap. Refrigerate until very cold, at least 4 hours or up to 3 days.

Pour the cold peach-cream mixture into an ice cream maker and churn according to the manufacturer's instructions. As soon as the ice cream has finished churning, spoon half of it into a freezer-safe container. Top with dollops of the reserved raspberry mixture, using about half of it, and stir gently in a figure-eight motion to swirl the raspberry mixture into the ice cream (page 104). Repeat to swirl together the remaining ice cream and raspberry mixture. Place parchment or waxed paper directly on the surface. Cover tightly and freeze until firm, at least 2 hours or up to 3 days.

chocolate–peanut butter ice cream

Here, a classic flavor pairing is brought to life in an easy-to-make ice cream. Natural peanut butter is preferred for this recipe because it has an intense peanut flavor and little or no sugar added. Be sure to stir it vigorously before using to incorporate any oil on the top.

6 tablespoons unsalted butter, at room temperature

¾ cup confectioners' sugar

¾ cup crunchy natural peanut butter

3 tablespoons heavy cream

1 batch Chocolate Ice Cream (page 20)

MAKES ABOUT 1¾ QUARTS

In a bowl, combine the butter, confectioners' sugar, peanut butter, and cream. Using an electric mixer on medium-high speed, beat until the mixture is light and fluffy, about 5 minutes, scraping down the sides of the bowl as needed. Use right away, or spoon into an airtight container and refrigerate for up to 3 days. (If refrigerated, let the peanut-butter mixture stand at room temperature for about 1 hour to soften before using.)

As soon as the ice cream has finished churning, spoon half of it into a freezer-safe container. Top with dollops of the reserved peanut-butter mixture, using about half of it, and stir gently in a figure-eight motion to swirl the mixture into the ice cream (page 104). Repeat to swirl together the remaining ice cream and peanut butter mixture. Place parchment or waxed paper directly on the surface. Cover tightly and freeze until firm, at least 2 hours or up to 3 days.

cinnamon–brown sugar ice cream

Using both whole cinnamon sticks and ground cinnamon intensifies the flavor in this ice cream, which is reminiscent of home-baked treats. Five cinnamon sticks or $\frac{1}{2}$ teaspoon ground cinnamon can be substituted if you only have one or the other in your pantry.

2 cups heavy cream

1$\frac{1}{2}$ cups whole milk

4 cinnamon sticks

$\frac{1}{8}$ teaspoon ground cinnamon

5 large egg yolks

$\frac{2}{3}$ cup packed light brown sugar

Pinch salt

MAKES ABOUT 1$\frac{1}{2}$ QUARTS

In a heavy saucepan, combine the cream; milk; cinnamon sticks, broken into pieces; and ground cinnamon. Warm over medium-high heat, stirring occasionally, until the mixture barely comes to a simmer, about 5 minutes. Meanwhile, in a heatproof bowl, combine the egg yolks, brown sugar, and salt. Whisk vigorously until the mixture lightens in color and doubles in volume, about 2 minutes.

Remove the cream mixture from the heat. Whisking constantly, slowly pour about 1 cup of the warm cream mixture into the egg mixture and whisk until smooth. Pour the resulting egg-cream mixture back into the saucepan, whisking constantly, and place over medium heat. Using a wooden spoon, stir until the mixture forms a custard thick enough to coat the back of the spoon (page 103), 1–2 minutes. Do not let it boil.

Meanwhile, set up an ice bath (page 103) in a large bowl and nest a smaller heatproof bowl inside. Pour the custard through a fine-mesh sieve into the smaller bowl; stir occasionally until cool. Remove the bowl from the ice bath and cover with plastic wrap. Refrigerate until very cold, at least 4 hours or up to 3 days.

Pour the cold custard into an ice cream maker and churn according to the manufacturer's instructions. Spoon the ice cream into a freezer-safe container and place parchment or waxed paper directly on the surface. Cover tightly and freeze until firm, at least 2 hours or up to 3 days.

chocolate-flecked fresh mint ice cream

Using fresh mint as opposed to mint extract adds a bright flavor to this ice cream. Instead of using large chocolate chunks, which can be both hard to bite into and difficult to scoop, the chocolate is finely grated, creating thin shards that melt easily when you eat the ice cream.

1¾ cups heavy cream

1½ cups whole milk

¾ cup fresh mint leaves

4 large egg yolks

¾ cup sugar

⅛ teaspoon salt

2 drops green food coloring (optional)

5 ounces bittersweet chocolate, finely grated

MAKES ABOUT 1 QUART

ice cream sandwiches

Make this delicious ice cream even better by placing a scoop between two chocolate wafers and pressing down gently to form a sandwich. For a special treat, you can also roll the edges of the sandwich in miniature chocolate chips.

In a heavy saucepan, combine the cream, milk, and mint leaves. Warm over medium-high heat, stirring occasionally, until the mixture barely comes to a simmer, about 5 minutes. Meanwhile, in a heatproof bowl, combine the egg yolks, sugar, and salt. Whisk vigorously until the mixture lightens in color and doubles in volume, about 2 minutes.

Remove the cream mixture from the heat. Whisking constantly, slowly pour about 1 cup of the warm cream mixture into the egg mixture and whisk until smooth. Pour the resulting egg-cream mixture back into the saucepan, whisking constantly, and place over medium heat. Using a wooden spoon, stir until the mixture forms a custard thick enough to coat the back of the spoon (page 103), 1–2 minutes. Do not let it boil.

Meanwhile, set up an ice bath (page 103) in a large bowl and nest a smaller heatproof bowl inside. Pour the custard through a fine-mesh sieve into the smaller bowl; stir occasionally until cool. Remove the bowl from the ice bath; stir in the food coloring, if using; and cover with plastic wrap. Refrigerate until very cold, at least 4 hours or up to 3 days.

Pour the cold custard into an ice cream maker and churn according to the manufacturer's instructions. Add the grated chocolate during the last minute of churning. Spoon the ice cream into a freezer-safe container and place parchment or waxed paper directly on the surface. Cover tightly and freeze until firm, at least 2 hours or up to 3 days.

almond toffee crunch ice cream

With its caramel flavor and crunchy texture, this ice cream is reminiscent of crème brûlée. Homemade almond toffee is easy to make and adds a buttery richness to the dessert. Other nuts, such as hazelnuts, macadamia nuts, or pecans can be substituted for the almonds.

1 cup sliced almonds

4 tablespoons unsalted butter, melted

3 tablespoons packed light brown sugar

1 teaspoon vanilla extract

1/8 teaspoon salt

2 ounces bittersweet chocolate, finely chopped

1 batch Smooth Vanilla Ice Cream (page 19)

MAKES ABOUT 1 1/2 QUARTS

Position a rack in the middle of the oven and preheat to 350°F. Line a rimmed baking sheet with parchment paper.

To make the almond toffee, in a bowl, stir together the sliced almonds, butter, brown sugar, vanilla, and salt. Spread the mixture in an even layer on the lined baking sheet. Bake until the almonds are evenly golden brown, about 12 minutes, rotating the baking sheet halfway through the baking time. Place the sheet on a wire rack and let the toffee cool completely, about 30 minutes.

Meanwhile, place the chocolate in the top of a double boiler or in a heatproof bowl set over (not touching) a saucepan of simmering water; stir the chocolate frequently until melted and smooth. Remove the bowl from the saucepan and let the chocolate cool slightly.

Using a spoon, drizzle the melted chocolate evenly over the cooled toffee. Refrigerate just until the chocolate is firm, about 10 minutes, then break the toffee into small pieces. Use the toffee right away, or store in an airtight container in the refrigerator for up to 1 day.

Churn the ice cream according to the manufacturer's instructions, adding the toffee pieces to the ice cream maker during the last minute of churning. Spoon the ice cream into a freezer-safe container and place parchment or waxed paper directly on the surface. Cover tightly and freeze until firm, at least 2 hours or up to 3 days.

peppermint ice cream

The best quality peppermint candies are usually available only around the winter holiday season, so plan on making this ice cream during the cold months of the year. You can also substitute small spearmint candies in place of the peppermints, if desired, or use a mixture.

30 small peppermint candies

1 cup whole milk

²⁄₃ cup sugar

¹⁄₄ teaspoon salt

2 cups heavy cream

MAKES ABOUT 1½ QUARTS

In a food processor, pulse the peppermint candies until they are finely crushed. Place half of the crushed candy in a small bowl and set aside. Place the remaining crushed candies in a saucepan and add the milk, sugar, and salt. Cook over medium-high heat, stirring occasionally, until the sugar and most of the candy are dissolved, about 5 minutes. Pour into a bowl and let cool to room temperature.

Stir the heavy cream into the milk mixture. Cover and refrigerate until very cold, at least 2 hours or up to 1 day.

Pour the cold cream-candy mixture into an ice cream maker and churn according to the manufacturer's instructions. Add the reserved crushed candies to the ice cream maker during the last minute of churning. Spoon the ice cream into a freezer-safe container and place parchment or waxed paper directly on the surface. Cover tightly and freeze until firm, at least 2 hours or up to 3 days.

white chocolate gelato

White chocolate is very sweet, so it pairs nicely with tart fruit compotes (see below) and tangy sauces. Adding the white chocolate to the custard base speeds up the cooking time, so watch the custard carefully as it cooks and take extra care that it doesn't burn.

2½ cups whole milk

5 large egg yolks

⅔ cup sugar

½ teaspoon vanilla extract

¼ teaspoon salt

7 ounces white chocolate, finely chopped

MAKES ABOUT 1 QUART

white chocolate–cranberry bowls

Serve this gelato with Cranberry Confiture (page 98) around the winter holiday season for a festive dessert. To dress it up, spoon dollops of the confiture into stemmed glasses, then place a scoop of the gelato on top of the confiture.

In a heavy saucepan over medium-high heat, gently warm the milk, stirring occasionally, until it barely comes to a simmer, about 5 minutes. Meanwhile, in a heatproof bowl, combine the egg yolks, sugar, vanilla, and salt. Whisk vigorously until the mixture lightens in color and doubles in volume, about 2 minutes.

Remove the milk from the heat. Whisking constantly, slowly pour about 1 cup of the warm milk into the egg mixture and whisk until smooth. Pour the resulting egg-milk mixture back into the saucepan, whisking constantly, and place over medium heat. Add the white chocolate, and using a wooden spoon, stir until the chocolate is completely melted and the mixture forms a custard thick enough to coat the back of the spoon (page 103), 1–2 minutes. Do not let it boil.

Meanwhile, set up an ice bath (page 103) in a large bowl and nest a smaller heatproof bowl inside. Pour the custard through a fine-mesh sieve into the smaller bowl; stir occasionally until cool. Remove the bowl from the ice bath and cover with plastic wrap. Refrigerate until very cold, at least 4 hours or up to 3 days.

Pour the cold custard into an ice cream maker and churn according to the manufacturer's instructions. Spoon the gelato into a freezer-safe container and place parchment or waxed paper directly on the surface. Cover tightly and freeze until firm, at least 2 hours or up to 3 days.

modern ice creams & gelatos

meyer lemon–olive oil ice cream

Plenty of egg yolks and a deep golden olive oil tint this ice cream a beautiful pale yellow color. Warming the Meyer lemon zest with the cream and milk gives the custard a sweet, bright taste and a delicate perfume, and silky olive oil lends its unique flavor and luxurious mouthfeel.

1½ cups whole milk

1¼ cups heavy cream

Grated zest of 2 Meyer lemons

7 large egg yolks

⅔ cup sugar

Pinch salt

⅓ cup extra-virgin olive oil

MAKES ABOUT 1 QUART

lemon-pistachio parfaits

For an innovative, palate-pleasing treat, layer scoops of this ice cream in tall glasses and drizzle with additional olive oil. For a little crunch, top each serving with sugared pistachios (page 99). Long iced-tea spoons are the perfect utensils to ensure you get some olive oil in each bite.

In a heavy saucepan, combine the milk, cream, and lemon zest. Warm over medium-high heat, stirring occasionally, until the mixture barely comes to a simmer, about 5 minutes. Meanwhile, in a heatproof bowl, combine the egg yolks, sugar, and salt. Whisk vigorously until the mixture lightens in color and doubles in volume, about 2 minutes.

Remove the milk mixture from the heat. Whisking constantly, slowly pour about 1 cup of the warm milk mixture into the egg mixture and whisk until smooth. Pour the resulting egg-milk mixture back into the saucepan, whisking constantly, and place over medium heat. Using a wooden spoon, stir until the mixture forms a custard thick enough to coat the back of the spoon (page 103), 1–2 minutes. Do not let it boil.

Meanwhile, set up an ice bath (page 103) in a large bowl and nest a smaller heatproof bowl inside. Pour the custard through a fine-mesh sieve into the smaller bowl; stir occasionally until cool. Remove the bowl from the ice bath, stir in the olive oil, and cover with plastic wrap. Refrigerate until very cold, at least 4 hours or up to 3 days.

Pour the cold custard into an ice cream maker and churn according to the manufacturer's instructions. Spoon the ice cream into a freezer-safe container and place parchment or waxed paper directly on the surface. Cover tightly and freeze until firm, at least 2 hours or up to 3 days.

cherry–chocolate truffle ice cream

If you can find them, sour cherries can be substituted for the Bing cherries in this recipe: simply increase the sugar to $1/2$ cup. Delicious additions include toasted chopped almonds or toasted flaked coconut; if you are using them, add these ingredients during the last minute of churning.

3 cups Bing cherries (about 1$1/4$ pounds), pitted and coarsely chopped

$1/3$ cup sugar

1 tablespoon kirsch

1 teaspoon fresh lemon juice

$1/2$ cup heavy cream

Pinch salt

4 ounces semisweet chocolate, finely chopped

1 batch Smooth Vanilla Ice Cream (page 19)

MAKES ABOUT 2 QUARTS

In a small saucepan, combine the cherries, sugar, and kirsch. Cook over medium heat, stirring occasionally, until the cherries soften and the juice becomes syrupy, about 5 minutes. Stir in the lemon juice. Spoon into a bowl, cover, and refrigerate until cold, at least 1 hour or up to 1 day.

In another small saucepan, combine the cream and salt. Warm over medium-high heat until it just comes to a simmer. Remove the pan from the heat, add the chocolate, and let stand for about 3 minutes. Using a wooden spoon, stir until the chocolate is melted and the mixture is smooth. Let cool to room temperature. Use right away, or refrigerate in an airtight container for up to 3 days. (If refrigerated, soften the chocolate mixture in a heatproof bowl set over, but not touching, simmering water in a saucepan.)

As soon as the ice cream has finished churning, spoon half of it into a freezer-safe container. Top with dollops of the reserved cherry and chocolate truffle mixtures, using about half of each, and stir gently in a figure-eight motion to swirl the mixtures into the ice cream (page 104). Repeat to swirl together the remaining ice cream and cherry and chocolate mixtures. Place parchment or waxed paper directly on the surface. Cover tightly and freeze until firm, at least 2 hours or up to 3 days.

crisp chocolate cookie ice cream

For the crunchiest texture, eat this ice cream the same day you make it. After a couple of days, the cookies will soften and become cakelike—it's different, but still delicious! Your favorite cookie, homemade or purchased, can be substituted for the chocolate wafers.

2 cups whole milk

1 cup heavy cream

4 large egg yolks

¾ cup sugar

2 teaspoons vanilla extract

¼ teaspoon salt

1 cup crumbled chocolate wafer cookies

MAKES ABOUT 1 QUART

In a heavy saucepan, combine the milk and cream. Warm over medium-high heat, stirring occasionally, until the mixture barely comes to a simmer, about 5 minutes. Meanwhile, in a heatproof bowl, combine the egg yolks, sugar, vanilla, and salt. Whisk vigorously until the mixture lightens in color and doubles in volume, about 2 minutes.

Remove the milk mixture from the heat. Whisking constantly, slowly pour about 1 cup of the warm milk mixture into the egg mixture and whisk until smooth. Pour the resulting egg-milk mixture back into the saucepan, whisking constantly, and place over medium heat. Using a wooden spoon, stir until the mixture forms a custard and is thick enough to coat the back of the spoon (page 103), 1–2 minutes. Do not let it boil.

Meanwhile, set up an ice bath (page 103) in a large bowl and nest a smaller heatproof bowl inside. Pour the custard through a fine-mesh sieve into the smaller bowl; stir occasionally until cool. Remove the bowl from the ice bath and cover with plastic wrap. Refrigerate until very cold, at least 4 hours or up to 3 days.

Pour the cold custard into an ice cream maker and churn according to the manufacturer's instructions. Add the crumbled cookies during the last minute of churning. Spoon the ice cream into a freezer-safe container and place parchment or waxed paper directly on the surface. Cover tightly and freeze until firm, at least 2 hours or up to 3 days.

brown butter–pecan ice cream

Cooking butter until it turns a shade or two darker is a flavor-enhancing trick often used in savory cooking. Unusual in sweets, brown butter lends a nutty flavor and ultrarich texture to this innovative recipe. Toasting the pecans while making the brown butter helps the two flavors unite.

1½ cups heavy cream

1½ cups whole milk

5 large egg yolks

²/₃ cup sugar

1 teaspoon vanilla extract

Brown-Butter Pecans (below)

MAKES ABOUT 1½ QUARTS

brown-butter pecans

In a frying pan over medium heat, melt 4 tablespoons butter. Add 1 cup coarsely chopped pecans and stir until the nuts are toasted and the butter begins to turn golden, 3–4 minutes. Transfer the nuts and butter to a bowl and sprinkle with ¼ teaspoon salt. Cool to room temperature.

In a heavy saucepan, combine the cream and milk. Warm over medium-high heat, stirring occasionally, until the mixture barely comes to a simmer, about 5 minutes. Meanwhile, in a heatproof bowl, combine the egg yolks, sugar, and vanilla. Whisk vigorously until the mixture lightens in color and doubles in volume, about 2 minutes.

Remove the cream mixture from the heat. Whisking constantly, slowly pour about 1 cup of the warm cream mixture into the egg mixture and whisk until smooth. Pour the resulting egg-cream mixture back into the saucepan, whisking constantly, and place over medium heat. Using a wooden spoon, stir until the mixture forms a custard thick enough to coat the back of the spoon (page 103), 1–2 minutes. Do not let it boil.

Meanwhile, set up an ice bath (page 103) in a large bowl and nest a smaller heatproof bowl inside. Pour the custard through a fine-mesh sieve into the smaller bowl; stir occasionally until cool. Remove the bowl from the ice bath and cover with plastic wrap. Refrigerate until very cold, at least 4 hours or up to 3 days.

Pour the cold custard into an ice cream maker and churn according to the manufacturer's instructions. Add the Brown-Butter Pecans during the last minute of churning. Spoon the ice cream into a freezer-safe container and place parchment or waxed paper directly on the surface. Cover tightly and freeze until firm, at least 2 hours or up to 3 days.

coconut-rum–toasted cashew ice cream

Creamy coconut, fiery dark rum, and crunchy cashews combine in this delightfully rich (and decidedly adult) ice cream. Look for cream of coconut—a thicker, sweeter product than coconut milk—near the cocktail mixers in most grocery stores or liquor stores.

¾ cup sweetened shredded coconut

1 can (14 ounces) unsweetened coconut milk

¾ cup cream of coconut

¾ cup heavy cream

¼ cup sugar

1 tablespoon dark rum

⅛ teaspoon salt

¾ cup salted roasted cashews, coarsely chopped

MAKES ABOUT 1 QUART

Position a rack in the middle of the oven and preheat to 350°F. Spread the shredded coconut on a baking sheet and bake until lightly browned, about 8 minutes, rotating the sheet and stirring the coconut halfway through the baking time. Let the coconut cool completely before using.

In a bowl, whisk together the coconut milk, cream of coconut, heavy cream, sugar, rum, and salt. Cover and refrigerate until very cold, at least 2 hours or up to 1 day.

Pour the cold coconut-cream mixture into an ice cream maker and churn according to the manufacturer's instructions. Add the cashews and toasted shredded coconut during the last minute of churning. Spoon the ice cream into a freezer-safe container and place parchment or waxed paper directly on the surface. Cover tightly and freeze until firm, at least 2 hours or up to 3 days.

mascarpone-hazelnut gelato

The richness of this gelato comes from the high amount of butterfat in the marscapone cheese that is used in place of the usual egg yolks. The creamy, semisweet base is the perfect showcase for the intensely nutty hazelnuts in this Italian-influenced treat.

1 cup hazelnuts

1 cup milk

1 cup heavy cream

¾ cup sugar

¾ pound mascarpone cheese

½ teaspoon vanilla extract

Pinch salt

MAKES ABOUT 1 QUART

sundaes for grown-ups

Top this gelato with Hot Fudge Sauce (page 92), Marshmallow Cream Topping (page 97), and toasted hazelnuts for a delicious adult sundae.

Preheat the oven to 350°F. Spread the hazelnuts on a rimmed baking sheet and bake until golden, about 10 minutes, rotating the sheet about halfway through the baking time. While the nuts are still warm, rub them with a kitchen towel to remove the skins. Let cool completely.

In a blender or food processor, combine the toasted hazelnuts, milk, cream, sugar, mascarpone, vanilla, and salt and blend until smooth. Pour into a bowl, cover, and refrigerate until very cold, at least 2 hours or up to 1 day.

Pour the cold toasted hazelnut–cream mixture into an ice cream maker and churn according to the manufacturer's instructions. As soon as it looks like softly whipped cream, remove the gelato from the ice cream maker; mascarpone can become grainy if overwhipped. Serve right away or spoon the gelato into a freezer-safe container and place parchment or waxed paper directly on the surface. Cover tightly and freeze until firm, at least 2 hours or up to 3 days.

jasmine tea ice cream with chocolate slivers

The floral flavor of jasmine tea pairs nicely with bittersweet chocolate. If you can't find jasmine tea pearls, you can use 3 jasmine tea bags: Heat the half-and-half and cream until they come to a simmer; remove from the heat, add the tea bags, and steep for 5 minutes. Discard the tea bags.

2 cups half-and-half

1½ cups heavy cream

1 tablespoon jasmine tea pearls

4 large egg yolks

¾ cup sugar

Pinch salt

Chocolate Slivers (below)

MAKES ABOUT 1 QUART

chocolate slivers

Melt 4 ounces chopped semisweet chocolate. Pour the melted chocolate onto a parchment-lined baking sheet and use an offset spatula to spread it into a very thin layer. Refrigerate until firm, about 10 minutes. Peel the chocolate from the parchment and break it into bite-sized pieces. Refrigerate until ready to use.

In a heavy saucepan, combine the half-and-half, cream, and jasmine pearls. Warm over medium-high heat, stirring occasionally, until the mixture barely comes to a simmer, about 5 minutes. Meanwhile, in a heatproof bowl, combine the egg yolks, sugar, and salt. Whisk vigorously until the mixture lightens in color and doubles in volume, about 2 minutes.

Remove the cream mixture from the heat. Whisking constantly, slowly pour about 1 cup of the warm cream mixture into the egg mixture and whisk until smooth. Pour the resulting egg-cream mixture back into the saucepan, whisking constantly, and place over medium heat. Using a wooden spoon, stir until the mixture forms a custard thick enough to coat the back of the spoon (page 103), 1–2 minutes. Do not let it boil.

Meanwhile, set up an ice bath (page 103) in a large bowl and nest a smaller heatproof bowl inside. Pour the custard through a fine-mesh sieve into the smaller bowl; stir occasionally until cool. Remove the bowl from the ice bath and cover with plastic wrap. Refrigerate until very cold, at least 4 hours or up to 3 days.

Pour the cold custard into an ice cream maker and churn according to the manufacturer's instructions. Add the Chocolate Slivers during the last minute of churning. Spoon the ice cream into a freezer-safe container and place parchment or waxed paper directly on the surface. Cover tightly and freeze until firm, at least 2 hours or up to 3 days.

spicy chocolate ice cream

The intense flavor of this ice cream comes from using two types of chocolate and hot chiles, which add a surprising kick. Cinnamon sticks and star anise pods also contribute hints of spice. Brown sugar, instead of granulated sugar, gives the ice cream an even deeper flavor.

1¾ cups heavy cream

1½ cups whole milk

2 dried red chiles, stemmed and seeded, or ¼ teaspoon cayenne pepper

3 cinnamon sticks

3 star anise pods

4 large egg yolks

⅔ cup packed light brown sugar

2 teaspoons vanilla extract

¼ teaspoon salt

4 ounces bittersweet chocolate, finely chopped

1 ounce unsweetened chocolate, finely chopped

MAKES ABOUT 1 QUART

In a heavy saucepan, combine the cream, milk, dried chiles, cinnamon sticks, and star anise pods. Warm over medium-high heat, stirring occasionally, until the mixture barely comes to a simmer, about 5 minutes. Meanwhile, in a heatproof bowl, combine the egg yolks, brown sugar, vanilla, and salt. Whisk vigorously until the mixture lightens in color and doubles in volume, about 2 minutes.

Remove the cream mixture from the heat. Whisking constantly, slowly pour about 1 cup of the warm cream mixture into the egg mixture and whisk until smooth. Pour the resulting egg-cream mixture back into the saucepan, whisking constantly, and place over medium heat. Add the bittersweet and unsweetened chocolates. Using a wooden spoon, stir until the chocolate has melted and the mixture forms a custard thick enough to coat the back of the spoon (page 103), 1–2 minutes. Do not let it boil.

Meanwhile, set up an ice bath (page 103) in a large bowl and nest a smaller heatproof bowl inside. Pour the custard through a fine-mesh sieve into the smaller bowl; stir occasionally until cool. Remove the bowl from the ice bath and cover with plastic wrap. Refrigerate until very cold, at least 4 hours or up to 3 days.

Pour the cold custard into an ice cream maker and churn according to the manufacturer's instructions. Spoon the ice cream into a freezer-safe container and place parchment or waxed paper directly on the surface. Cover tightly and freeze until firm, at least 2 hours or up to 3 days.

salted caramel ice cream

This ice cream has a lot of buttery-sweet caramel flavor and just a hint of saltiness, bringing a pleasing savory twist to a favorite dessert. Fine sea salt, added here in the custard base, is preferred over other types of salt for its fresh-from-the-sea flavor and lack of additives.

1⅓ cups sugar

4 tablespoons salted butter

1½ cups heavy cream

1½ cups milk

6 large egg yolks

1 teaspoon vanilla extract

¾ teaspoon fine sea salt

MAKES ABOUT 1 QUART

salted caramel sundaes

To add an extra punch of sweet-salty flavor, top bowlfuls of this ice cream with Caramel Sauce (page 94) and sprinkle with coarse, flaky sea salt.

In a heavy saucepan, cook the sugar over medium-high heat until it begins to melt, about 5 minutes. Continue to cook, stirring, until the sugar is melted and turns golden amber in color, about 3 minutes. Stirring constantly, carefully add the butter, cream, and milk. Reduce the heat to medium and continue to cook, stirring, until the mixture is completely melted and returns to a bare simmer, about 5 minutes. Meanwhile, in a heatproof bowl, combine the egg yolks, vanilla, and salt. Whisk vigorously until the mixture lightens in color and doubles in volume, about 2 minutes.

Remove the cream mixture from the heat. Whisking constantly, slowly pour about 1 cup of the warm cream mixture into the egg mixture and whisk until smooth. Pour the resulting egg-cream mixture back into the saucepan, whisking constantly, and place over medium heat. Using a wooden spoon, stir until the mixture forms a custard thick enough to coat the back of the spoon (page 103), 1–2 minutes. Do not let it boil.

Meanwhile, set up an ice bath (page 103) in a large bowl and nest a smaller heatproof bowl inside. Pour the custard through a fine-mesh sieve into the smaller bowl; stir occasionally until cool. Remove the bowl from the ice bath and cover with plastic wrap. Refrigerate until very cold, at least 4 hours or up to 3 days.

Pour the cold custard into an ice cream maker and churn according to the manufacturer's instructions. Spoon the ice cream into a freezer-safe container and place parchment or waxed paper directly on the surface. Cover tightly and freeze until firm, at least 2 hours or up to 3 days.

plum & port wine ice cream

Port's dried fruit flavor is a delicious complement to summer-fresh plums, and it turns this ice cream a delightful mauve color. When in season, you can substitute figs for the plums for a slightly sweeter treat; they will cook in the same amount of time as the plums.

2 cups ruby Port

²/₃ cup sugar

1 pound ripe red plums, halved and pitted

Pinch salt

1 cup half-and-half

1 cup heavy cream

MAKES ABOUT 1 QUART

In a heavy saucepan, combine the Port and sugar and bring to a boil over medium-high heat. Reduce the heat to low and add the plums and salt. Cook until the plums begin to soften and the Port has reduced to about ³/₄ cup, about 20 minutes. Let cool to room temperature.

Pour the cooled plum mixture into a blender or food processor. Add the half-and-half and blend until very smooth. Pour the plum mixture into a bowl and stir in the cream. Cover and refrigerate until very cold, at least 2 hours or up to 1 day.

Pour the cold plum mixture into an ice cream maker and churn according to the manufacturer's instructions. Spoon the ice cream into a freezer-safe container and place parchment or waxed paper directly on the surface. Cover tightly and freeze until firm, at least 2 hours or up to 3 days.

ice cream cups with crunchy cookies

Serve this ice cream in small soup cups with Almond Biscotti (page 91). The buttery, crisp biscuits pair nicely with the sweet-tart combination of plums and Port.

orange-cardamom ice cream

Whole cardamom pods and orange zest are infused into a rich custard base for an elegant spiced ice cream. This is the perfect finale for a dinner party—the flavor is sophisticated yet the dessert can be made days in advance. Garnish servings with candied orange peel (page 100).

2 cups heavy cream

1½ cups whole milk

2 tablespoons cardamom pods, toasted (see below) and crushed with a heavy saucepan

Grated zest of 1 orange

5 large egg yolks

¾ cup sugar

¼ teaspoon salt

MAKES ABOUT 1½ QUARTS

toasted cardamom pods

Toasting the cardamom pods before crushing them enhances the spice's earthy flavor. In a dry frying pan over medium-low heat, toast the cardamom pods, tossing frequently, until fragrant, about 2 minutes. Transfer to a plate and let cool completely.

In a heavy saucepan, combine the cream, milk, toasted crushed cardamom pods, and orange zest. Warm over medium-high heat, stirring occasionally, until the mixture barely comes to a simmer, about 5 minutes. Meanwhile, in a heatproof bowl, combine the egg yolks, sugar, and salt. Whisk vigorously until the mixture lightens in color and doubles in volume, about 2 minutes.

Remove the cream mixture from the heat. Whisking constantly, slowly pour about 1 cup of the warm cream mixture into the egg mixture and whisk until smooth. Pour the resulting egg-cream mixture back into the saucepan, whisking constantly, and place over medium heat. Using a wooden spoon, stir until the mixture forms a custard thick enough to coat the back of the spoon (page 103), 1–2 minutes. Do not let it boil.

Meanwhile, set up an ice bath (page 103) in a large bowl and nest a smaller heatproof bowl inside. Pour the custard through a fine-mesh sieve into the smaller bowl; stir occasionally until cool. Remove from the ice bath and cover with plastic wrap. Refrigerate until very cold, at least 4 hours or up to 3 days.

Pour the cold custard into an ice cream maker and churn according to the manufacturer's instructions. Spoon the ice cream into a freezer-safe container and place parchment or waxed paper directly on the surface. Cover tightly and freeze until firm, at least 2 hours or up to 3 days.

chocolate malted ice cream

Classic soda-fountain flavors combine in this ice cream, satisfying the child in all of us. Malted milk powder is easy to find at most grocery stores; look for it in the baking aisle. Milk powder is very sweet, so a minimal amount of sugar is called for in the recipe.

1½ cups whole milk

1½ cups heavy cream

½ cup malted milk powder or chocolate malt powder

4 large egg yolks

⅓ cup sugar

2 tablespoons unsweetened cocoa powder

¼ teaspoon salt

5 ounces milk chocolate, finely chopped

MAKES ABOUT 1 QUART

In a heavy saucepan, combine the milk, cream, and malted milk powder. Warm over medium-high heat, stirring occasionally, until the mixture barely comes to a simmer, about 5 minutes. Meanwhile, in a bowl, combine the egg yolks, sugar, cocoa powder, and salt. Whisk vigorously until the mixture lightens in color and doubles in volume, about 2 minutes.

Remove the milk mixture from the heat. Whisking constantly, slowly pour about 1 cup of the milk mixture into the egg mixture and whisk until smooth. Pour the resulting egg-milk mixture back into the saucepan, whisking constantly, and place over medium heat. Add the chopped chocolate. Using a wooden spoon, stir until the chocolate has completely melted and the mixture forms a custard thick enough to coat the back of the spoon (page 103), 1–2 minutes. Do not let it boil.

Meanwhile, set up an ice bath (page 103) in a large bowl and nest a smaller heatproof bowl inside. Pour the custard through a fine-mesh sieve into the smaller bowl; stir occasionally until cool. Remove the bowl from the ice bath and cover with plastic wrap. Refrigerate until very cold, at least 4 hours or up to 3 days.

Pour the cold custard into an ice cream maker and churn according to the manufacturer's instructions. Spoon the ice cream into a freezer-safe container and place parchment or waxed paper directly on the surface. Cover tightly and freeze until firm, at least 2 hours or up to 3 days.

avocado ice cream

Naturally creamy in texture and pleasantly nutty in flavor, avocados are the featured ingredient in this lightly sweetened ice cream. It's so alluring, even the skeptics won't be able to resist a scoop. Try it served over sliced mangoes or papaya with a squeeze of fresh lime juice.

1 pound ripe avocados
(about 3)

1½ cups half-and-half

¾ cup sugar

2 tablespoons fresh lime juice

¼ teaspoon sea salt

1 cup heavy cream

MAKES ABOUT 1 QUART

Halve and pit the avocados. Scoop the avocado flesh into a blender or food processor and add the half-and-half, sugar, lime juice, and salt. Blend until smooth. Pour the avocado mixture into a bowl and whisk in the cream.

Nest the bowl with the avocado mixture in an ice bath (page 103) and stir until cool, about 30 minutes; it is important to chill the avocado mixture well to prevent discoloration.

Pour the cool avocado mixture into an ice cream maker and churn according to the manufacturer's instructions. Spoon the ice cream into a freezer-safe container and place parchment or waxed paper directly on the surface. Cover tightly and freeze until firm, at least 2 hours or up to 3 days.

lavender ice cream with honeyed pine nuts

A popular herb in the south of France, lavender can be used in both sweet and savory recipes. Here it stars in a rich custard base, which helps showcase the herb's unique floral flavor and aroma. If using fresh lavender, use half as much as the dried, or about 1½ teaspoons.

2 cups half-and-half

1 cup heavy cream

1 tablespoon dried organic lavender blossoms

4 large egg yolks

½ cup sugar

¼ cup wildflower honey

¼ teaspoon salt

Honeyed Pine Nuts (below)

MAKES ABOUT 1½ QUARTS

honeyed pine nuts

In a small frying pan over medium heat, toast ½ cup pine nuts, stirring, until golden, about 5 minutes. Stir in 2 tablespoons honey, 1 tablespoon water, and 1 teaspoon unsalted butter. Cook, stirring, until the mixture has thickened, about 1 minute. Pour onto a plate and cool completely.

In a heavy saucepan, combine the half-and-half, cream, and lavender. Warm over medium-high heat, stirring occasionally, until the mixture barely comes to a simmer, about 5 minutes. Meanwhile, in a heatproof bowl, combine the egg yolks, sugar, honey, and salt. Whisk vigorously until the mixture lightens in color and doubles in volume, about 2 minutes.

Remove the cream mixture from the heat. Whisking constantly, slowly pour about 1 cup of the cream mixture into the egg mixture and whisk until smooth. Pour the resulting egg-cream mixture back into the saucepan, whisking constantly, and place over medium heat. Using a wooden spoon, stir until the mixture forms a custard thick enough to coat the back of the spoon (page 103), 1–2 minutes. Do not let it boil.

Meanwhile, set up an ice bath (page 103) in a large bowl and nest a smaller heatproof bowl inside. Pour the custard through a fine-mesh sieve into the smaller bowl; stir occasionally until cool. Remove the bowl from the ice bath and cover with plastic wrap. Refrigerate until very cold, at least 4 hours or up to 3 days.

Pour the cold custard into an ice cream maker and churn according to the manufacturer's instructions. Add the Honeyed Pine Nuts during the last minute of churning. Spoon the ice cream into a freezer-safe container and place parchment or waxed paper directly on the surface. Cover tightly and freeze until firm, at least 2 hours or up to 3 days.

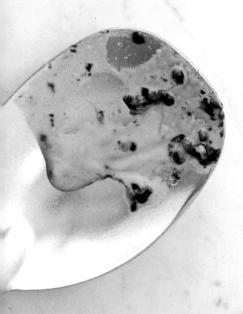

frozen yogurts & sherbets

honey–poppy seed frozen yogurt

Lightly tangy yogurt, floral honey, and crunchy poppy seeds combine in this easy-to-prepare frozen treat. A touch of heavy cream lends richness to the frozen yogurt base, while grated lemon zest and a pinch of salt help these somewhat subtle flavors shine.

3 cups plain whole-milk yogurt

1 cup heavy cream

¾ cup wildflower or clover honey

Grated zest of 1 lemon

1 tablespoon poppy seeds

Pinch salt

MAKES ABOUT 1 QUART

In a bowl, whisk together the yogurt, cream, honey, lemon zest, poppy seeds, and salt until smooth. Cover and refrigerate until very cold, at least 2 hours or up to 1 day.

Pour the cold yogurt mixture into an ice cream maker and churn according to the manufacturer's instructions. Spoon the frozen yogurt into a freezer-safe container and place parchment or waxed paper directly on the surface. Cover tightly and freeze until firm, at least 2 hours or up to 3 days.

frozen yogurt–topped grilled fruit

For a midsummer treat, serve this frozen yogurt with grilled stone fruits, such as nectarines, plums, or cherries. Grill halved, pitted fruit over medium-high heat for 3–4 minutes per side, or until the fruit is nicely marked by the grill but is not dried out. Place a few pieces of the grilled fruit in each serving bowl, drizzle with honey, and top with some of the frozen yogurt.

banana-maple frozen yogurt

Using bananas in frozen treats is delicious, yet can be somewhat tricky—you must work quickly so that the fruit doesn't turn brown. Here, maple syrup acts as a sweetener while lending its unique flavor to the fruity frozen yogurt. For extra maple flavor, drizzle servings with additional syrup.

2 firm but ripe bananas (about 1 pound total weight), peeled

2 cups Greek-style plain whole-milk yogurt

1 cup maple syrup, preferably grade A

½ cup heavy cream

2 teaspoons fresh lemon juice

Pinch salt

MAKES ABOUT 1 QUART

In a blender or food processor, combine the bananas, yogurt, maple syrup, cream, lemon juice, and salt. Blend until very smooth. Pour the banana-yogurt mixture into a bowl.

Nest the bowl with the yogurt mixture in an ice bath (page 103) and stir occasionally until very cold, about 20 minutes. It is important to chill the mixture well to prevent discoloration.

Pour the cold yogurt mixture into an ice cream maker and churn according to the manufacturer's instructions. Spoon the frozen yogurt into a freezer-safe container and place parchment or waxed paper directly on the surface. Cover tightly and freeze until firm, at least 2 hours or up to 3 days.

banana frozen yogurt sundae

For a quick treat with all the flavors of a banana split, top this frozen yogurt with Hot Fudge Sauce (page 92), Vanilla Whipped Cream (page 79), and a cherry.

vanilla frozen yogurt with summer berry swirl

High-quality yogurt enhanced with just the right amount of sweetener and pure vanilla extract provides the base for this summery delight. Here, instead of spooning berries on top, the berries are crushed and then swirled into the yogurt to spread their fruity flavor throughout.

4 cups plain whole-milk yogurt

²/₃ cup plus 2 tablespoons sugar

¼ cup light corn syrup

2 tablespoons vanilla extract

Pinch salt

½ cup raspberries

½ cup blueberries

½ cup blackberries

1 teaspoon fresh lemon juice

MAKES ABOUT 1½ QUARTS

In a bowl, whisk together the yogurt, the ²/₃ cup sugar, corn syrup, vanilla, and salt. Cover and refrigerate until very cold, at least 2 hours or up to 1 day.

In another bowl, combine the raspberries, blueberries, blackberries, lemon juice, and the remaining 2 tablespoons sugar. With a fork, lightly crush the berries until they release some of their juices. Cover the mixture and refrigerate until ready to use.

Pour the cold yogurt mixture into an ice cream maker and churn according to the manufacturer's instructions. As soon as the frozen yogurt has finished churning, spoon half of it into a freezer-safe container. Top with dollops of the reserved berry mixture, using about half of it, and stir gently in a figure-eight motion to swirl the mixture into the yogurt (page 104). Repeat to swirl together the remaining frozen yogurt and berrry mixture. Place parchment or waxed paper directly on the surface. Cover tightly and freeze until firm, at least 2 hours or up to 3 days.

frozen yogurt–granola parfaits

A perfect dessert for a weekend brunch, layer this frozen yogurt with your favorite granola in a tall, narrow glasses. The parfaits can be assembled up to 4 hours ahead of time, covered, and kept in the freezer. Top with whipped cream and fresh berries just before serving.

strawberry–crème fraîche sherbet

Sherbet is usually made with heavy cream or milk blended with a fruit purée. In this version, crème fraîche replaces the milk or cream, adding a welcome tang to complement the sweet strawberries. A touch of fresh lemon juice helps draw out the berry flavor.

3 cups (1½ pints) strawberries, hulled

2 tablespoons sugar

1 cup crème fraîche

½ cup light corn syrup

2 teaspoons fresh lemon juice

Pinch salt

MAKES ABOUT 1 QUART

In a bowl, combine the strawberries and sugar and lightly crush with a fork. Whisk in the crème fraîche, corn syrup, lemon juice, and salt. Cover and refrigerate until very cold, at least 2 hours or up to 1 day.

Pour the cold strawberry mixture into an ice cream maker and churn according to the manufacturer's instructions. Spoon the sherbet into a freezer-safe container and place parchment or waxed paper directly on the surface. Cover tightly and freeze until firm, at least 2 hours or up to 3 days.

tangerine-cream sherbet

This sherbet uses the flavors of a classic childhood ice pop and turns them into a sophisticated dessert, bright with the flavor of fresh tangerines. Look for tangerines during the winter months, when they proliferate in local markets. Mandarins or clementines can be substituted.

1 cup heavy cream

1 cup crème fraîche

½ cup light corn syrup

½ cup sugar

Finely grated zest of 2 tangerines

2 cups fresh tangerine juice (from about 10 tangerines)

Pinch salt

MAKES ABOUT 1 QUART

In a bowl, whisk together the cream, crème fraîche, corn syrup, sugar, tangerine zest and juice, and salt. Cover and refrigerate until very cold, at least 2 hours or up to 1 day.

Pour the cold tangerine mixture into an ice cream maker and churn according to the manufacturer's instructions. Spoon the sherbet into a freezer-safe container and place parchment or waxed paper directly on the surface. Cover tightly and freeze until firm, at least 2 hours or up to 3 days.

tangerine-cream float

In a small saucepan, combine 2 cups freshly squeezed tangerine juice (from about 10 tangerines) and 1½ cups sugar. Bring to a boil over medium-high heat and cook, stirring occasionally, until the sugar dissolves to make a tangerine simple syrup. Transfer to a bowl, cover, and refrigerate until cold, at least 1 hour. To assemble the float, place a couple of scoops of the sherbet in a tall glass, then add ¼ cup of the cooled tangerine syrup and 1½ cups cold club soda. Serve with a long iced-tea spoon.

key lime sherbet

Tiny, sweet Key limes shine in this sherbet, offset by a measure of tangy sour cream. If you can't find Key limes, conventional limes can be substituted; they are not as sweet, though, so add 2 tablespoons sugar to the saucepan with the water to compensate for their tartness.

¾ cup sugar

Finely grated zest of 6 Key limes

½ cup fresh Key lime juice (from about 12 Key limes)

1½ cups half-and-half

½ cup sour cream

Pinch salt

MAKES ABOUT 1 QUART

In a saucepan, combine the sugar and ¾ cup water. Bring to a boil over medium-high heat, stirring occasionally until the sugar is completely dissolved and a syrup is formed. Let cool to room temperature.

In a bowl, whisk together the lime zest and juice, half-and-half, sour cream, salt, and cooled sugar syrup. Cover and refrigerate until very cold, at least 2 hours or up to 1 day.

Pour the cold lime mixture into an ice cream maker and churn according to the manufacturer's instructions. Spoon the sherbet into a freezer-safe container and place parchment or waxed paper directly on the surface. Cover tightly and freeze until firm, at least 2 hours or up to 3 days.

sorbets & granitas

melon sorbet

This refreshing sorbet showcases melons at their summer best. Choose from the sweetest-smelling melon varieties at the market or just pick your favorite. For a refreshing twist, add $1/4$ cup loosely packed spearmint leaves to the food processor while puréeing the melon mixture.

$3/4$ cup sugar

4 cups diced ripe melon (from about 1 small melon)

1 tablespoon fresh lemon juice

Pinch salt

MAKES ABOUT 1$1/2$ QUARTS

melon sorbet medley

Churn batches of three different sorbet flavors such as cantaloupe, honeydew, and watermelon, and then use a small scoop to create a colorful bowl of frozen delights. Small sorbet balls can also be made into pops for whimsical single-serving portions (see page 25).

In a small saucepan, combine the sugar and $3/4$ cup water. Bring to a boil over medium-high heat, stirring occasionally until the sugar is completely dissolved and a syrup is formed. Let cool to room temperature.

Pour the cooled syrup into a blender or food processor. Add the melon, lemon juice and salt and blend until very smooth. Pour into a bowl, cover, and refrigerate until very cold, at least 2 hours or up to 1 day.

Pour the cold melon purée into an ice cream maker and churn according to the manufacturer's instructions. Spoon the sorbet into a freezer-safe container and place parchment or waxed paper directly on the surface. Cover tightly and freeze until firm, at least 2 hours or up to 3 days.

strawberry-basil sorbet

The licorice-like flavor of basil is a perfect match for strawberries in the springtime. Other herbs, such as mint or lemon verbena, can be substituted for the basil. These herbs are a bit more potent than basil, so use half as much, or about 2 tablespoons torn or roughly chopped leaves.

3 cups (1 1/2 pints) strawberries, hulled and cut in half

2/3 cup sugar

1/4 cup fresh basil leaves, torn into small pieces or roughly chopped

2 teaspoons fresh lemon juice

Pinch salt

MAKES ABOUT 1 QUART

In a bowl, stir together the strawberries, sugar, and basil leaves. Cover and let stand at room temperature until the berries release some of their juices and the sugar is completely dissolved, about 30 minutes.

Pour the strawberry mixture into a blender or food processor. Add the lemon juice and salt and blend until very smooth. Transfer the blended fruit to a bowl, cover, and refrigerate until cold, at least 2 hours or up to 1 day.

Pour the cold strawberry purée into an ice cream maker and churn according to the manufacturer's instructions. Spoon the sorbet into a freezer-safe container and place parchment or waxed paper directly on the surface. Cover tightly and freeze until firm, at least 2 hours or up to 3 days.

mango-ginger sorbet

The pungent, spicy flavor of fresh ginger enhances the tropical sweetness of mango in this sorbet. Serve it at the end of an Asian- or Indian-themed meal for a fitting finale. You can garnish with crystallized ginger, cut into slivers, for a beautiful presentation.

¾ cup sugar

2 ripe mangoes (about 2 pounds total weight)

1 tablespoon peeled and grated fresh ginger (do not substitute ground ginger)

2 tablespoons fresh lime juice

Pinch salt

MAKES ABOUT 1 QUART

mango-ginger gelato

Transform this sorbet into a gelato by whisking ¾ cup heavy cream into the mango purée before churning.

In a small saucepan, combine the sugar and ¾ cup water. Bring to a boil over medium-high heat, stirring occasionally until the sugar is completely dissolved and a syrup is formed. Let cool to room temperature.

Peel and dice the mangoes, discarding the pits. Place the diced mango in a blender or food processor and add the cooled syrup, ginger, lime juice, and salt. Blend until very smooth. Pour into a bowl, cover, and refrigerate until very cold, at least 2 hours or up to 1 day.

Pour the cold mango purée into an ice cream maker and churn according to the manufacturer's instructions. Spoon the sorbet into a freezer-safe container and place parchment or waxed paper directly on the surface. Cover tightly and freeze until firm, at least 2 hours or up to 3 days.

champagne sorbet

Cooking the Champagne slightly before churning it into a sorbet will create a firmer texture and a more concentrated flavor. The icy texture of the sorbet will mimic the effervescence of sparkling wine, adding to the dessert's refreshing quality. You can also use a nonalcoholic sparkling wine.

1 cup sugar

2 cups Champagne or sparkling wine

1 tablespoon fresh lemon juice

Pinch salt

MAKES ABOUT 1 QUART

In a saucepan, combine the sugar and 1 cup water. Bring to a boil over medium-high heat, stirring occasionally. Add the Champagne and continue to cook at a bare simmer for 2 minutes. Remove from heat and pour into a bowl. Stir in 1 cup cold water, the lemon juice, and the salt.

Nest the bowl with the Champagne mixture in an ice bath (page 103) and stir until cool. Remove from the ice bath, cover, and refrigerate until very cold, at least 4 hours or up to 1 day.

Pour the cold Champagne mixture into an ice cream maker and churn according to the manufacturer's instructions. Spoon the sorbet into a freezer-safe container and place parchment or waxed paper directly on the surface. Cover tightly and freeze until firm, at least 2 hours or up to 3 days.

vietnamese coffee granita

Vietnamese coffee is typically served with sweetened condensed milk over ice. Here, the coffee itself is transformed into "ice," which is then served over the thick, sugary milk and topped with a dollop of whipped cream. Try it as an innovative dessert for a Southeast Asian meal.

3 cups freshly brewed hot coffee

¼ cup sugar

½ cup sweetened condensed milk

Vanilla Whipped Cream (below), for serving (optional)

MAKES ABOUT 1 QUART

vanilla whipped cream

In a deep bowl, combine ¾ cup well-chilled heavy cream, 2 tablespoons sugar, and ½ teaspoon vanilla extract. Using a mixer on high speed, beat until the cream is billowy and soft peaks form, about 2 minutes. Cover and refrigerate until ready to use.

In a wide, shallow dish that will easily fit into the freezer, combine the coffee, sugar, and 1½ cups water. Whisk to dissolve the sugar. Freeze the mixture until a thin layer of ice forms around the edges and on top, about 2 hours.

Using a fork, rake the mixture, breaking up the solid portions into fine flakes of ice. Return the mixture to the freezer and continue to freeze for 2–3 hours longer, scraping the ice crystals with the fork to break them up every 30 minutes.

If the granita freezes too firmly, remove it from the freezer and let stand at room temperature to soften for 10 minutes, then scrape with the fork until the ice crystals are of even size and return the granita to the freezer. Spoon the finished granita into a freezer-safe container, cover tightly, and freeze for up to 3 days.

To serve, divide the condensed milk evenly among each of 4 serving glasses, and then spoon the granita into the glasses. Top with a dollop of Vanilla Whipped Cream, if desired.

pomegranate ice

High-quality pomegranate juice is readily available in markets today. Its lightly sweet, slightly peppery flavor makes an intriguing dessert, brightened by a touch of fresh lime juice. Try it in bowls topped with fresh pomegranate seeds, or make it into ice pops (below).

¾ cup sugar

3 cups pure pomegranate juice

Pinch salt

1 tablespoon fresh lime juice

MAKES ABOUT 1 QUART

pomegranate ice pops

Instead of pouring the pomegranate mixture into a shallow dish, pour it into ice-pop molds and freeze until solid, at least 4 hours or up to 3 days. Makes 6–8 ice pops.

In a small saucepan, combine the sugar and ½ cup water. Bring to a boil over medium-high heat, stirring occasionally until the sugar is completely dissolved and a syrup forms. Let cool to room temperature.

Pour the syrup into a bowl and stir in the pomegranate juice, salt, and lime juice. Cover and refrigerate until very cold, at least 2 hours or up to 1 day.

Pour the cold pomegranate mixture into a wide, shallow dish that will easily fit into the freezer. Freeze until a thin layer of ice forms around the edges and on top, about 1 hour. Using a fork, rake the mixture, breaking up the solid portions into fine flakes of ice. Return the mixture to the freezer and continue to freeze for 2–3 hours longer, scraping the ice crystals with the fork to break them up every 30 minutes.

If the ice freezes too firmly, remove it from the freezer and let stand at room temperature to soften for 10 minutes, then scrape with the fork until the ice crystals are of even size and return the ice to the freezer. Spoon the finished ice into a freezer-safe container, cover tightly, and freeze for up to 3 days.

blackberry-wine ice

Fruit-infused wine ice makes a delightful palate cleanser between courses at an elegant dinner or a light finale on a warm summer night. Other berries such as raspberries or blueberries can be substituted for the blackberries. This ice pairs nicely with a flute of crisp sparkling wine.

½ cup sugar

½ cup fruity red wine such as Pinot Noir

4 cups (2 pints) blackberries

2 tablespoons fresh orange juice

Pinch salt

MAKES ABOUT 1 QUART

blackberry-wine sorbet

To make a smooth-textured sorbet, pour the blackberry-wine mixture into an ice cream maker and follow the manufacturer's instructions for churning.

In a small saucepan, combine the sugar and ½ cup water. Bring to a boil over medium-high heat, stirring occasionally until the sugar is completely dissolved and a syrup forms. Add the wine and continue to cook for 1 minute. Let cool to room temperature.

Pour the cooled wine syrup into a blender or food processor. Add the blackberries, orange juice, and salt and blend until very smooth. Press the mixture through a fine-mesh sieve into a bowl to remove the berry seeds. Cover and refrigerate until very cold, at least 2 hours or up to 1 day.

Pour the blackberry-wine mixture into a wide, shallow dish that will easily fit into the freezer. Freeze until a thin layer of ice forms around the edges and on top, about 1 hour. Using a fork, rake the mixture, breaking up the solid portions into fine flakes of ice. Return the mixture to the freezer and continue to freeze for 2–3 hours longer, scraping the ice crystals with the fork to break them up every 30 minutes.

If the ice freezes too firmly, remove it from the freezer and let stand at room temperature to soften for 10 minutes, then scrape with the fork until the ice crystals are of even size and return the ice to the freezer. Spoon the finished ice into a freezer-safe container, cover tightly, and freeze for up to 3 days.

blood orange granita

Blood oranges are only available for a few months in the late winter and early spring. When squeezed, their crimson-colored juice produces a gorgeous granita. Serve it with a dollop of Vanilla Whipped Cream (page 79) for a refreshing dessert.

Finely grated zest from 2 blood oranges

¾ cup sugar

1¾ cups fresh blood orange juice (from about 6 blood oranges)

Pinch salt

2 teaspoons orange liqueur, such as Grand Marnier or triple sec

MAKES ABOUT 1 QUART

Combine the blood orange zest, sugar, and ¾ cup water in a small saucepan. Bring to a boil over medium-high heat, stirring occasionally until the sugar is completely dissolved and a syrup forms, about 5 minutes. Let cool to room temperature.

Pour the cooled syrup into a wide, shallow dish that will easily fit in the freezer. Stir in the blood orange juice, salt, and orange liqueur.

Freeze the mixture until a thin layer of ice forms around the edges and on top, about 1 hour. Using a fork, rake the mixture, breaking up the solid portions into fine flakes of ice. Return the mixture to the freezer and continue to freeze for 2–3 hours longer, scraping the ice crystals with the fork to break them up every 30 minutes.

If the granita freezes too firmly, remove it from the freezer and let stand at room temperature to soften for 10 minutes, then scrape with the fork until the ice crystals are of even size and return the granita to the freezer. Spoon the finished granita into a freezer-safe container, cover tightly, and freeze for up to 3 days.

cones, cookies & toppings

waffle cones

The easiest way to make waffle cones is by using a machine specifically made for the job. Waffle cone makers are inexpensive and worth it for the cone connoisseur. Most come with a cone mold to make shaping them a snap. A pizelle iron can be used instead.

2 large eggs

⅓ cup granulated sugar

⅓ cup packed light brown sugar

4 tablespoons unsalted butter, melted

¼ teaspoon salt

2 teaspoons vanilla extract

¾ cup all-purpose flour

MAKES ABOUT 12 CONES

In a bowl, combine the eggs and granulated and brown sugars. Whisk vigorously until the mixture lightens in color and is smooth, about 1 minute. Whisk in the melted butter, salt, vanilla, and flour until completely combined. Cover and refrigerate for at least 30 minutes or up to 3 days before using.

Make the cones in a waffle cone maker according to the manufacturer's instructions. Cool completely on a wire rack. Use right away, or store in an airtight container at room temperature for up to 3 days.

waffle cups

To make waffle cups, follow the manufacturer's instructions for making waffle cones, adding about half the amount of batter to the iron as directed. Remove the baked waffle round from the iron and carefully drape it over the outside of an overturned bowl, pressing it to the sides of the bowl; it's okay if the sides pinch together or buckle. Let the waffle cup cool on the bowl until firm. Repeat with the remaining batter.

tuile cookies

These delicate cookies are the perfect crunchy partner for a bowl of ice cream or other frozen treat. You can use two cookies to make a sandwich or use one cookie as a base on which to build a composed dessert. You can also make delicious cookie cups (below left) from the same batter.

4 tablespoons unsalted butter

¼ cup light corn syrup

¼ cup sugar

¼ cup all-purpose flour

Pinch salt

MAKES ABOUT 12 COOKIES

tuile cookie cups

As soon as the cookies come out of the oven, use a small offset spatula to lift each cookie off the sheet and carefully press into the cups of a muffin pan. Let cool in the pan to room temperature, and then carefully remove the cookie cups.

Position a rack in the middle of the oven and preheat to 350°F. Line 3 large baking sheets with silicone baking mats or parchment paper.

In a saucepan, combine the butter, corn syrup, and sugar. Bring to a boil over medium heat, stirring occasionally, until the sugar dissolves. Remove from the heat and whisk in the flour and salt until combined. Let cool completely, about 30 minutes.

Use a measuring tablespoon, scoop a heaping spoonful of the batter from the saucepan and drop onto one of the prepared baking sheets. Repeat, filling each baking sheet with 4 evenly spaced scoops of batter. Bake the cookies 1 sheet at a time, until golden, about 10 minutes. Let cool just until the edges are set, 1–2 minutes. Using an offset spatula, transfer the cookies to a wire rack and cool completely.

Serve the cookies right away, or carefully place in an airtight container and store at room temperature for up to 3 days.

chocolate chip cookies

There's no better accompaniment to a bowl of ice cream or other frozen treat than a warm, homemade chocolate chip cookie. You can also use the cookies to make ice-cream sandwiches—either full-sized or miniature—for frozen delights you can eat out of hand.

1 1/3 cups all-purpose flour

1/2 teaspoon baking powder

1/2 teaspoon baking soda

1/2 teaspoon salt

1/2 cup unsalted butter, at room temperature

1/2 cup granulated sugar

1/2 cup firmly packed light brown sugar

1 large egg

1 teaspoon vanilla extract

1 cup semisweet chocolate chips

MAKES ABOUT 48 COOKIES

Preheat the oven to 350°F. In a bowl, stir together the flour, baking powder, baking soda, and salt and set aside.

Using an electric mixture on high speed, beat the butter until fluffy and pale yellow. Add the granulated and brown sugars and continue beating until the mixture is well blended, about 1 minute. Add the egg and vanilla and beat on low speed until completely incorporated, scraping down the sides of the bowl with a rubber spatula as needed.

Add the flour mixture to the butter-sugar mixture and mix on low speed just until blended. Use a wooden spoon to stir in the chocolate chips.

Drop rounded tablespoons of the dough onto 2 ungreased baking sheets, spacing the cookies about 2 inches apart.

Bake the cookies until golden brown around the edges and lightly golden in the center, about 12 minutes, rotating the sheets halfway through baking. Let the cookies cool briefly on the pans on wire racks for about 5 minutes, and then transfer the cookies directly to the racks and let cool completely.

brownies

A chewy, fudgy brownie alongside ice cream, gelato, or frozen yogurt is a real treat. This recipe is intensely chocolaty because it uses chocolate in the batter and is then studded with chocolate chips before baking. Other kinds of chips or candy chunks can also be used.

½ cup unsalted butter, cut into 4 pieces

3 ounces unsweetened chocolate, finely chopped

1 cup sugar

Pinch salt

2 large eggs, at room temperature

1 teaspoon vanilla extract

¾ cup cake flour

¾ cup semisweet chocolate chips

MAKES 16 BROWNIES

Preheat the oven to 350°F. Lightly grease an 8-inch-square baking pan.

In a heatproof bowl, combine the butter and chopped chocolate. Set the bowl over (but not touching) simmering water in a saucepan and stir occasionally until melted, about 4 minutes. Add the sugar and salt and stir well with a wooden spoon. Add the eggs and vanilla and stir until well blended. Sift the flour over the mixture and stir until just blended. Stir in the chocolate chips.

Pour the batter into the prepared pan, spreading it evenly and smoothing the top with a long, thin spatula. Bake the brownies until a toothpick inserted into the center comes out almost clean, about 35 minutes. Let the brownies cool completely in the pan on a wire rack.

When ready to serve, cut into 16 small squares and lift out the brownies with an offset spatula.

almond biscotti

These biscotti are delicious served with fruit, nut, and spiced ice creams and gelatos, such as Pistachio Gelato (page 25), Plum & Port Wine Ice Cream (page 52), and Orange-Cardamom Ice Cream (page 54). They are also the perfect accompaniment to a simple cup of coffee.

2 cups all-purpose flour

1½ teaspoons baking powder

½ teaspoon salt

¾ cup unsalted butter, at room temperature

¾ cup sugar

2 large eggs

1 teaspoon vanilla extract

1 cup almonds, toasted

MAKES 32 BISCOTTI

Position a rack in the middle of the oven and preheat to 350°F. Line 2 large baking sheets with parchment paper.

In a bowl, whisk together the flour, baking powder, and salt. In a large bowl, combine the butter and sugar, and using an electric mixer on medium speed, beat until well blended, about 1 minute. Add the eggs and vanilla and beat on low speed until blended, scraping down the sides of the bowl with a spatula as needed. Slowly add the flour mixture and beat on low speed just until blended. Add the toasted almonds and beat until mixed.

Divide the dough in half. Using lightly moistened hands, gently press one half of the dough into a 10-by-2½-inch rectangular log on a prepared baking sheet. Repeat to shape the remaining dough half on the second sheet. Bake until the edges are light brown and the tops feel firm, 17–20 minutes, switching the position of the sheets halfway through baking. When done, let the logs stand on the baking sheets for about 10 minutes. Reduce the oven temperature to 325°F.

Using a serrated knife, cut each log into 16 slices ½–¾ inch wide. Place the slices, cut sides down, in a single layer on the baking sheets. Bake until the outsides of the cookies are crisp and the edges are dark golden brown, about 20 minutes more.

Let the biscotti cool on the baking sheets for 5 minutes, then transfer to wire racks and let cool completely. Serve right away, or place in an airtight container and store at room temperature for up to 1 week.

hot fudge sauce

Warm, gooey chocolate sauce poured over vanilla ice cream is the ultimate simple pleasure, but the deep, rich, chocolaty flavor enhances a variety of frozen treats as well. Try it with Peppermint Ice Cream (page 33) or Marscapone-Hazelnut Gelato (page 46).

$\frac{2}{3}$ cup heavy cream

$\frac{1}{2}$ cup light corn syrup

2 tablespoons firmly packed dark brown sugar

5 ounces bittersweet chocolate, coarsely chopped

Pinch salt

1 teaspoon vanilla extract

MAKES ABOUT 2 CUPS

In a heavy saucepan, combine the cream, corn syrup, and brown sugar. Bring to a boil over medium-low heat, stirring occasionally until the sugar is dissolved, about 5 minutes.

In a heatproof bowl, combine the chopped chocolate and salt. Pour the hot cream mixture over the chocolate and stir with a heatproof silicone spatula until the chocolate is melted and smooth. Stir in the vanilla.

Use right away, or cover and refrigerate for up to 3 days. Reheat gently over low heat before serving (you may need to thin it with a little cream).

caramel sauce

Silky, buttery caramel sauce poured on almost anything is divine. Or, try swirling this sauce into vanilla or chocolate ice cream during the last few minutes of churning. You can turn this into salted caramel sauce by using 1 teaspoon coarse sea salt in place of the pinch of salt in the recipe.

1^1/$_2$ cups sugar

1^1/$_4$ cups heavy cream

Pinch salt

MAKES ABOUT 2^1/$_2$ CUPS

In a heavy, high-sided saucepan, cook the sugar over medium-high heat until it begins to melt around the edges, about 5 minutes. Continue to cook, stirring with a wooden spoon, until the sugar is melted and turns golden amber in color, about 3 minutes longer.

Carefully pour the cream down the side of the pan in a slow, steady stream (it will bubble and spatter), stirring constantly until completely smooth. Stir in the salt. Pour the caramel sauce into a small heatproof bowl and let cool completely before using.

Use right away, or cover and store in the refrigerator for up to 1 week. Bring the sauce to room temperature before serving.

fresh strawberry topping

This is a great sauce to make in the spring and summer when strawberries are at their peak. Blending most of the strawberry mixture until smooth, then augmenting it with a chopped berry mixture, produces a sauce that coats frozen desserts evenly but also has juicy berry bits.

4 cups (2 pints) strawberries, hulled and coarsely chopped

1/3 cup sugar

1 teaspoon fresh lemon juice

MAKES ABOUT 3 CUPS

In a bowl, stir together the strawberries, sugar, and lemon juice. Spoon all but 1/2 cup of the strawberry mixture into a blender and blend until smooth. Stir the strawberry purée into the reserved chopped strawberry mixture. Use right away, or cover and store in the refrigerator for up to 3 days.

marshmallow cream topping

This sweet, fluffy topping is a crowd-pleasing favorite. For a deconstructed rocky road ice cream, spoon dollops of this onto scoops of Chocolate Ice Cream (page 20) and sprinkle with chopped nuts. For a decadent topping, swirl the marshmallow cream with Hot Fudge Sauce (page 92).

2 large egg whites

1 cup miniature marshmallows

1 cup sugar

¼ cup light corn syrup

½ teaspoon cream of tartar

Pinch salt

1 teaspoon vanilla extract

MAKES ABOUT 5 CUPS

In a large, clean, heatproof bowl, combine the egg whites, marshmallows, sugar, 6 tablespoons water, the corn syrup, cream of tartar, and salt. Set the bowl over (but not touching) simmering water in a saucepan and whisk constantly until the sugar and marshmallows have dissolved and the mixture is very warm to the touch (about 160°F on an instant-read thermometer), about 3 minutes. Remove the bowl from the saucepan.

Using an electric mixer on medium-high speed, beat the mixture until soft peaks form, about 2 minutes. Reduce the mixer speed to low and beat in the vanilla. Use right away.

cranberry confiture

This tart fruit topping, accented by lively orange flavor, makes a great accompaniment to White Chocolate Gelato (page 34) or other very sweet ice creams, gelatos, and frozen yogurts. If you don't have a cinnamon stick, you can substitute ¼ teaspoon ground cinnamon.

½ pound fresh or frozen cranberries

Grated zest and juice of 1 orange

⅓ cup sugar

1 cinnamon stick

Pinch salt

Pinch freshly grated nutmeg

MAKES ABOUT 2 CUPS

In a small saucepan, combine the cranberries, orange zest and juice, sugar, cinnamon stick, salt, and nutmeg. Cook over medium heat, stirring occasionally, until the cranberries burst and and the juice thickens to the consistency of syrup, 10–12 minutes. Pour the cranberry mixture into a small heatproof bowl and let cool completely, stirring occasionally. Remove and discard the cinnamon stick.

Use right away or cover and store in the refrigerator for up to 1 week.

sugared nuts

There's a reason why nuts are part of the classic ice cream sundae: They add crunchy texture and a little flavor-enhancing salt to an otherwise smooth, sweet dessert. In place of the walnuts here, you can use cashews, almonds, shelled pistachios, or a mixture of your favorite nuts.

2 cups walnut halves

3 tablespoons sugar

Pinch salt

2$\frac{1}{2}$ tablespoons unsalted butter, cut into pieces

MAKES ABOUT 2 CUPS

Preheat the oven to 350°F. In a bowl, toss together the nuts, sugar, and salt. Spread the mixture in a single layer on a rimmed baking sheet. Scatter the butter pieces over the nuts and stir gently to mix. Bake, stirring the nuts and shaking the pan several times, until lightly browned, 10–12 minutes. If you prefer darker, toastier nuts, bake them 2–3 minutes longer.

Transfer the nuts to a clean baking sheet and let cool completely. Use right away or store in an airtight container at room temperature for up to 3 days.

candied citrus peel

Candied citrus peel dresses up any dessert, but is especially nice as a garnish for simply flavored ice creams, gelatos, frozen yogurts, and fruit sorbets. Try it, too, as a topping for citrus-based desserts; the sugared rind adds a sweet-bitter kick to intensify the featured flavor.

3 large, thick-skinned lemons, 4 limes, or 2 oranges

3 cups sugar

MAKES ABOUT 1 CUP

Using a citrus zester, remove the peel from the citrus fruits, being careful not to remove too much of the white pith along with the peel. Reserve the fruit for another use.

Bring a saucepan three-fourths full of water to a boil over high heat. Add the citrus peel and boil for 4 minutes. Drain the peel and rinse under cold water. Repeat this step once more, using fresh water; this removes the bitterness from any pith attached to the peel.

In a saucepan, combine 2 cups of the sugar, 1½ cups water, and the prepared citrus peel. Bring to a simmer over medium-low heat and cook until the peel is soft and translucent, about 30 minutes. Let the peel cool to room temperature in the syrup.

Using a slotted spoon or tongs, transfer the citrus peel to a wire rack set over a rimmed baking sheet; discard the syrup. Let the peel stand until it feels only slightly tacky to the touch, about 2 hours.

Spread the remaining 1 cup sugar in a shallow dish. Toss the peel in the sugar until all of the pieces are completely coated. Use right away, or transfer to an airtight container and store at room temperature for up to 5 days.

making a custard base

1 In a heavy saucepan, combine the dairy product(s) (cream, milk, or half-and-half), and flavorings (vanilla beans or nuts). Warm over medium-high heat, stirring occasionally, until just barely simmering, about 5 minutes. Meanwhile, in a heatproof bowl, combine the egg yolks, sweetener, salt, and any other flavorings called for in the recipe and whisk vigorously until the mixture lightens in color and doubles in volume, about 2 minutes.

2 Remove the dairy mixture from the heat. Slowly pour about 1 cup of the hot dairy mixture into the egg mixture, whisking constantly. Pour the resulting warmed egg-dairy mixture back into the saucepan with the rest of the dairy mixture. This process of slowly warming the eggs is called *tempering;* it prevents the eggs from scrambling when they must be combined with hot liquid.

3 Place the saucepan with the egg-dairy mixture over medium heat and cook, stirring constantly with a wooden spoon, until the mixture forms a custard thick enough to coat the back of the spoon, 1–2 minutes. While stirring, make sure to reach all areas on the bottom and sides of the saucepan to ensure that the custard doesn't scorch or curdle. Also, do not let it boil. The custard is done when it coats the back of a spoon and a finger drawn along the spoon leaves a trail that does not fill in immediately. Remove the custard from the heat.

4 It's best to set up the ice bath before you start cooking the custard so that the cooking can be halted immediately. Fill a large mixing bowl half full with ice cubes and cold water. Nestle a smaller heatproof bowl inside. Set a fine mesh sieve over the smaller bowl. When the custard has finished cooking, pour it through the sieve, pressing the liquid through with the back of the spoon. Leave behind and discard any grainy solids or other ingredients, like a vanilla bean pod, cinnamon stick, or coffee beans. Cool the custard, stirring occasionally, until chilled to the touch, 30–45 minutes.

making swirled frozen treats

1 As soon as the frozen dessert has finished churning, spoon half of it into a freezer-safe container. Using a large tablespoon, spoon dollops of the swirling mixture on top of the frozen dessert, using about half of it. If you are swirling with more than one mixture, alternate with dollops of each.

2 Next, dip the spoon into the center of one of the dollops, and working in a figure-eight motion, stir until the swirling mixture is evenly distributed throughout, but not completely incorporated into, the frozen dessert. Repeat step 1, spooning the remaining frozen dessert into the container, topping with the remaining swirling mixture, and swirling the two elements together.

working with vanilla beans

1 Using a sharp paring knife, and holding the tip of the vanilla bean on the board, cut the vanilla bean in half lengthwise, stopping just short of the tip. It's okay if you split the bean entirely, but leaving the bean intact allows you to scrape out the seeds in one step instead of two.

2 Rotate the vanilla bean so the cut sides are facing away from you and the attached tip is closest to you on the the board. Hold the attached tip to the board with your thumb. Holding the paring knife in your other hand and starting at the attached tip, scrape out the vanilla seeds using the back side of the knife. You may have to repeat this step a few times to scrape out all of the seeds.

mix & match!

There are endless possibilities for creative flavor pairings and composed desserts in this book. In addition to the serving suggestions in these pages, here are a few more winning combinations. But don't stop with these—use your imagination to create your own one-of-a-kind concoctions.

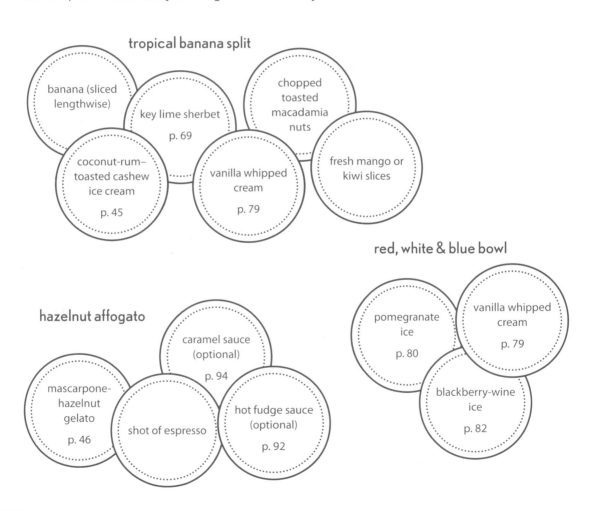

tropical banana split

banana (sliced lengthwise)

key lime sherbet
p. 69

chopped toasted macadamia nuts

coconut-rum–toasted cashew ice cream
p. 45

vanilla whipped cream
p. 79

fresh mango or kiwi slices

red, white & blue bowl

pomegranate ice
p. 80

vanilla whipped cream
p. 79

blackberry-wine ice
p. 82

hazelnut affogato

caramel sauce (optional)
p. 94

mascarpone-hazelnut gelato
p. 46

shot of espresso

hot fudge sauce (optional)
p. 92

neapolitan waffle bowls

- smooth vanilla ice cream — p. 19
- waffle cups — p. 87
- chocolate ice cream — p. 20
- strawberry ice cream — p. 23
- pistachio gelato (optional) — p. 25

berry delicious parfait

- strawberry–crème fraîche sherbet — p. 66
- fresh strawberry topping — p. 95
- vanilla whipped cream — p. 79
- fresh berries and toasted nuts

mango-ginger champagne float

- mango-ginger sorbet — p. 76
- champagne sorbet — p. 77
- champagne or sparkling wine

minty brownies à la mode

- brownies — p. 90
- hot fudge sauce — p. 92
- chocolate-flecked fresh mint ice cream — p. 31

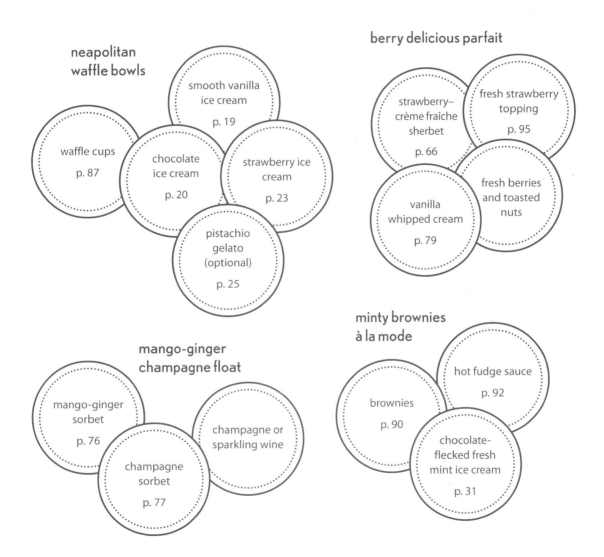

index

weldon**owen**

415 Jackson Street, Suite 200, San Francisco, CA 94111

Telephone: 415 291 0100 Fax: 415 291 8841

www.wopublishing.com

Weldon Owen is a division of

BONNIER

WELDON OWEN INC.

CEO and President Terry Newell

VP, Sales and Marketing Amy Kaneko

Director of Finance Mark Perrigo

VP and Publisher Hannah Rahill

Executive Editor Jennifer Newens

Associate Editor Julia Humes

VP and Creative Director Gaye Allen

Creative Director Emma Boys

Art Director Alexandra Zeigler

Senior Designer Ashley Martinez

Junior Designer Anna Grace

Production Director Chris Hemesath

Production Manager Michelle Duggan

Color Manager Teri Bell

SWEET SCOOPS

Conceived and produced by Weldon Owen Inc.

Copyright © 2010 Weldon Owen Inc.

Set in Nobel and Myriad Pro.

Color separations by Embassy Graphics

Printed and bound in China by 1010 Printing, Ltd.

First printed in 2010

10 9 8 7 6 5 4 3 2 1

Library of Congress Control Number: 2010938155

ISBN-13: 978-1-61628-068-0

ISBN-10: 1-61628-068-9

ACKNOWLEDGMENTS

Weldon Owen wishes to thank the following people for their generous support in producing this book:

Prop Stylist Leigh Noe; **Photographer's Assistant** Austin Goldin; **Food Stylist's Assistant** Ara Armstrong; **Copyeditor** Kate Washington; **Proofreaders** Kathryn Shedrick and Kate Washington; and **Indexer** Elizabeth Parson.